D1214728

A 782.42 YOU
Young, Neil.
Greendale /
Kiel Public Library
34270000538131

Original Map Illustration for Hard Cover Book: Neil Young
Art Direction & Design: Gary Burden & Jenice Heo for R. Twerk & Co.
Paintings Photographed by Joel Bernstein

Thanks: Elliot Rabinowitz, L.A. Johnson, Ralph Molina, Billy Talbot,
Frank Sampedro, Pegi Young, Susan Hall, Nancy Hall, Twink Brewer

©2004 Amber Jean Productions

Published by Sanctuary Publishing Limited
Sanctuary House, 45-53 Sinclair Road
London W14 0NS, United Kingdom
www.sanctuarypublishing.com
Text ©2004 Neil Young
Illustrations and Paintings ©2004 James Mazzeo

All rights reserved. No part of this book may be reproduced in any
form or by any electronic or mechanical means, including information
storage or retrieval systems, without permission in writing from the
publisher, except by a reviewer, who may quote brief passages.

ISBN: 1-86074-622-5
ISBN: 1-86074-649-7

Printed and Bound by Insync Media, Inglewood, CA
Printed on 30% PCW Domtar Recycled Paper using Soy Inks

greendale
neil young

illustrations by james mazzeo

Sanctuary

2/05

greendale

we're going on a little trip, folks....so, these songs are about a place called greendale and it's a green dale....there's a lot going on in town. it seems to be a pretty mellow place, really. in town, there's about 20 to 25,000 people and it's not a very big place at all....if there is a huge map, which there is, that just shows greendale, very little happening over here, there's mountains and farms, over there, there's an ocean....well, greendale is a nice town, but it has its quirks....there's a lot going on in greendale that i don't know about either. can you imagine? i mean, i made it up and i don't know what the hell is goin' on. so don't feel bad if you feel a little out of it with this. no one really knows....

A 782.42 YOU
Young, Neil.
Greendale /
Kiel Public Library
34270000538131

falling from above

i'm doing some new songs that i wrote awhile ago and this is chapter one. just didn't want to confuse you right out of the gate. gonna see how far i can take you here with this new material, just see what happens. i still remember my old songs....these songs are about a family that lives in a place called the double e rancho, outside of greendale, just a few miles down a little road up in the hills. the term "rancho" is spanish...."el rancho" kind of thing. it's a funny thing in america. spanish was there a long time ago, but still every once in awhile somebody writes down "rancho" just because it sounds cool. so that's what they did....it used to be called the double L, but now it's called the double E. it was a relatively easy change to make. earl green is a painter so he painted the sign, he added two lines. it's like a cow brand, y'know? how they have brands on ranches. the double L looked like that and earl and edith moved into the place and they were very clever, you know, earl just added two lines. we talked about how edith and earl renamed the double E and they almost made history. the locals rose up. they were mad as hell 'cause it used to be the double L. change comes slow in the country. i told you that a long time ago. i didn't expect you to remember, though, i really didn't, so i don't mind telling you again. grandpa likes to sit on the porch at the double E 'cause when the sun comes up in the morning it's very nice there, a good place to read the paper.

falling from above

grandpa said to cousin jed
sittin' on the porch
"i won't retire
but i might retread

seems like that guy singin' this song
been doin' it for a long time
is there anything he knows
that he ain't said?

sing a song for freedom
sing a song for love
sing a song for depressed angels
falling from above"

grandpa held the paper
pretendin' he could see
but he couldn't read without his glasses on

"how can all these people
afford so many things?
when i was young
people wore what they had on...and mama said

'a little love and affection
in everything you do
will make the world a better place
with or without you'"

a little love and affection
in everything you do

slammin' down a late night shot
the hero and the artist compared
goals and visions and afterthoughts
for the 21st century

but mostly came up with nothin'
so the truth was never learned
and the human race just kept rollin' on

rollin' through the fighting
rollin' through the religious wars
rollin' down the temple walls
and the church's exposed sores

rollin' through the fighting
the religious wars
mostly came up with nothin'

"grandpa, here's your glasses
you'll see much better now"
said that young girl of edith and earl's
but grandpa just kept starin'
he was lost in some distant thought
then he turned and said
to that young girl

"a little love and affection
in everything you do
will make the world a better place
with or without you"

with or without you
a better place
with or without you
with or without you

hear that rooster crowin'
down on the double e
it's a new morning
dawning on the green

bouncing off the towers
the sun's heading down for the streets
the business meeting
window shades are drawn

another morning edition
headed for the porch
because grandma puts down the paper
before grandpa raises his fork

a little love and affection
in everything you do
with or without you

hear the rooster crowin'
down on the double e

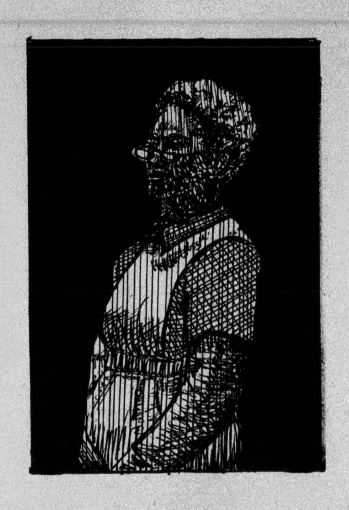

double e

there's a family that lives here on the rancho; this song is about the family that lives there. there is a nice girl there, about 18 or 19, her name is sun green and she lives with her mom and dad, earl and edith green. her cousin, jed green and grandma and grandpa green, they live in greendale but it's not too far, so they visit a lot. sun green is such a beautiful girl. grandpa is so proud of her. aside from carling, sun is really the only kid who's still left. she's gonna carry on somehow the green tradition, if not the green name, sun green. s-u-n green. names are funny in the green family. ciela green was the grandmother of sun. she had two daughters by two different green brothers. one of their names was sea, s-e-a and the other one was sky green....tonight earl and edith are headed out to a party at the bar, because edith loves to dance. sun loves to dance too, the good daughter. she's working on her homework though, working on a book report on a book called "how to use the media." she's also doing an essay on saving the wilderness. her favorite wilderness area is alaska, so she's focusing on the state of alaska in her essay. sun wants to be an artist, maybe a performance artist. she's working on something out in the field she wants a lot of people to see someday. she's working in hay. she carries bales of hay on the back of a flatbed truck out into the middle of the field on a green hillside and that's her canvas.

double e

back in the country
livin' on the double e
in the sunshine of her life
there's a ready young filly
and mom and daddy won't let her leave
mom and papa won't let her go

but when they go out dancin'
she breaks out on her own
she's hot enough to burn the house down
and mom and daddy don't know

when edith and earl
renamed the double e
they nearly made history
the neighbors rose up
and some of them were mad as hell
'cause it used to be the double L

change comes slow in the country
when you're new there's a lot of distrust
years pass by uneventful
and memories turn to dust

meanwhile granny
has got her bright colors on
with the sunshine in her eyes
cruisin' by the bars
and honky tonks where she met grandpa
and caught that young man's eye

awhile ago

dusty white eldorado
cruisin' through the trees
slippin' through the shadows
of what used to be

back in the day
livin' in the summer of love
livin' in the summer of love

grandma's ok
but not the same since grandpa's gone
she's livin' in the summer of love

back in the day
livin' in the summer of love
livin' in the summer of love

livin' in the summer of love

livin' in the summer of love

livin' in the summer of love

later

devil's sidewalk

greendale seems to be a pretty mellow place, really. not very big, but it's big enough. and there's a jail and satan lives in the jail. he's in every town, i think, but in this town he's in jail....but he doesn't have to stay there, he can just leave when he wants. he just walks through the wall. but he likes it in there....i think it's the people who were there before him or something, make him feel good. this song here is chapter 6, i think. and if i'm wrong about that, i can be corrected on the internet. but one thing is....and i hope i don't step on any religious feet here....but the devil lives in greendale. i don't think he's restricted to just greendale either. he lives in the jail in greendale that was built in 1911. it's a little box. it's very funky, just a small little box with bars. but he walks through walls and things, so it doesn't matter. he just likes it there....so captain green had to say a few things to the crew, down at the dock. there's a little harbor in greendale and there's a dock and it's an old wooden pier, falling down. they don't use it anymore but it's still there. it's gonna be condemned and torn down, but it's the last dock like it on the whole west coast. it's just a mess but it's still there. and there's a fishing house there on the end where they used to clean the fish and process them. a lot of things happen there in that little house, but i don't want to get into that right now. i want to tell you about captain john green, the brother of grandpa. he never goes into greendale. the closest he gets is the dock. he won't come in. but one day, he stood on the dock talking to his crew, who are a bunch of young kids, 19-year-olds, the helmsman and the mate....he only had two guys on his crew. he was talking to them, giving them some advice....i guess you could say, passing on some information.

devil's sidewalk

"when the red light shines
on the streets of hate
where the devil dines
who knows what he ate?

it's a simple thing
trying to stay afloat"
the captain said
without his boat

"some things are getting better
other things a little worse
it's a situation
much like a curse

it's the devil's sidewalk
it's the devil's door
i'd try to avoid it"
said the captain of the shore

"there's a garden growing
and a million weeds
with no way of knowing
who has done which deed"

"that's an honest tale"
said the helmsman to the mate
"about a woman delicious
and a matter of fate"

big wheel still rollin'
down on me
one thing i can tell you
is you got to be free

john lennon said that
and i believe in love
i believe in action
when push comes to shove

"who cares what you believe?"
said the captain amazed
"if you stood in my shoes
your eyes would be glazed"

so, my fair damsel
won't you take your leave?
are you headed for the country
where you wear the green sleeve

and the children laugh
and the old folks sing
and the church bell tolls
for a miraculous thing?

where the big red furnace
just glows and glows
where the big heart beats
where the big wheel rolls...

leave the driving

this is a story of how one stupid move can change your whole life. this song happens on the highway, on the way out of greendale. as a matter of fact, it happens right at the "leaving greendale" sign, where the map of greendale ends. there is no more greendale after that. the highway ends, everything ends at that point. the map....there is nothing else, just the map. cars driving down the road get to the "leaving greendale" sign and then they're off the map. that's where it happens. there's a beautiful map of greendale that's drawn by some old greendale person, i suppose. you know these maps where everything's flattened out, it's like you see it but it's on a big piece of paper. you see city hall and a little drawing of city hall. a very nice map. right at the end of the map, highway one, coast highway, right there on the edge is where this happens. cousin jed is driving his beautiful funky car down highway 1. just at the edge is where jed gets stopped by officer carmichael. that's where jed killed him. when i was writing this i had no idea what i was doing, so i was just as surprised as you are. jed went to jail and i guess he's still there. and you know who else is there. but remarkably, jed and the devil actually look very similar. but they say there's a little bit of the devil in everybody. but this resemblance is a little striking for me. it kinda reminds me of myself, actually. but from everything that happens in life, i've learned this and i'm at least 10, is that there's a lot of wreckage from some things and this cop, officer carmichael, he had a life.

leave the driving

out on the old coast highway
flyin' through the night
jed got stopped by the chp
for speedin' and no brake lights

rolled down the driver's window
slipped his gun down under the seat
glove box full of cocaine
trunk was full of weed

"driver's license and registration"
said the officer with his flashlight
searchin' around the floor of the car
smellin' like somethin' ain't right

jed's life flashed before him
like a black and white super 8
he heard the sound of the future
on a scratchy old 78

nothin' was still, all was movin'
when the flashlight found the gun
then jed pulled the trigger
in a split second tragic blunder

"makes you think about livin'
and what life has to tell"
said jed to grandpa
from inside his cell

camouflage hung in his closet
guns all over the wall
plans for buildings and engineers
and a book with no numbers at all

the whole town was stunned
they closed the coast highway for 12 hours
no one could believe it
jed was one of ours

meanwhile across the ocean
living in the internet
is the cause of an explosion
no one has heard yet

but there's no need to worry
there's no reason to fuss
just go on about your work now
and leave the driving to us

and we'll be watching you
no matter what you do
and you can do your part
by watching others too

grandpa put down the paper
staring in disbelief
jed had always been good to him
and never gave him any grief

"the moral of this story
is try not to get too old
the more time you spend on earth
the more you see unfold

and as an afterthought
this must too be told
some people have taken pure bullshit
and turned it into gold"

carmichael on the very edge of greendale, about a hundred yards from that sign that says "leaving greendale," there is a big billboard put up by the greendale chamber of commerce. that's where officer carmichael parked his police cruiser on that fateful day....so jed went to jail. he's in jail. he screwed up. he's had it. i don't think they're gonna get him. i took note of that comment over there. this is a test. i don't know if i'm gonna pass it or not. but i already passed that cortez test. i'd like to take it again someday, maybe today. but for a minute i'd like to stay in greendale because jed's in jail. okay. what about the wreckage of murder? it's terrible. jed killed a cop. and that's a bummer right there, because carmichael....officer carmichael....had a family, he had friends. he had a beautiful wife. officer carmichael is no longer on the planet. some people think that police are evil and hippies are good, but it may not be true. there's a gray area. he didn't have any kids, but he did have a nice group of friends, all the other officers who worked with him. he had a story to tell, but he's not around anymore, so i'll tell you a little bit about him and that's it. it's not worth it to spend too much time on him, since he doesn't have a future. carmichael had a terrible argument with his wife that morning as he was leaving to go to work. so that was kind of too bad, 'cause she never saw him again. so it makes you think about always try to be nice to the one you love because you never know what's gonna happen. so i learned that from this song. i don't care if you learn it, i learned it.

carmichael

a silk scarf and a napkin
hidden in a drawer
two hundred bucks in an envelope
labeled lenore

"maybe she shouldn't see this
she should never know"
said the widow's best friend anne
"i'll just take it and go

i'll give her the money later
say it was in his shoe
that way she'll never find out
that'll do"

"carmichael was a credit to the force
in everything he did
it's like we got a big hole in our side
where he fit

if any of you officers
would like to say a word
now would be the time
to be heard"

"thank you chief, i sure would
he was a partner of mine
he was always very careful
and played it straight down the line"

one by one the officers spoke
and the service drew to a close
he had no living relatives
but his wife who never showed

she just couldn't face the men
they all understood
they got in their cars and drove home
as directly as they could

"carmichael you asshole"
the new widow sobbed beneath her veil
"shot down in the line of duty
is this how justice never fails?

i wish that things were better
when we said goodbye today
but we had our share of good times, though
along the way

remember
'hey mr. las vegas
you used to be so cool!!'?
we met wayne newton down at pebble beach
and you acted like a fool

but we both just couldn't stop laughin'
it seemed so funny to us
we left our luggage back in the room
and almost missed the bus

that was a great vacation
maybe the best of all
but goddammit carmichael you're dead now
and i'm talkin' to the wall"

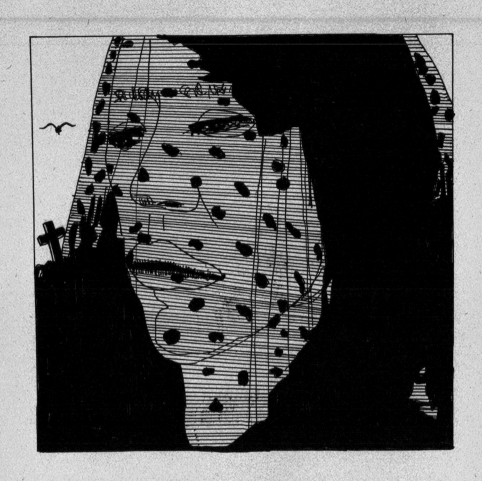

the force got back to normal
carmichael was replaced
for one year nobody parked a car
in carmichael's space

bandit this song has to do with earl green, sun green's father, edith green's husband, jed green's uncle (jed the cop killer). earl's an artist. he's always painting these beautiful paintings....and earl hardly ever sells a painting....so he's traveling around. he's got money problems and he likes to go in his camper, he's got a winnebago, like a camper you live in and drive around and he drives around to different galleries with his paintings in his winnebago, goes in to people and tries to get something happening. one night he stopped in a motel. he had a few personal moments with the computer and television set....

bandit

turnin' the pages
in this old book
seems familiar
might be worth a second look

wrappin' up dope in a paper bag
talkin' to yourself
takin' a drag
who are you kidding
with what you say?
what does it matter?
they'll never hear it anyway

got to get past
the negative thing
lawyers and business
you get what you bring
no one's sorry
you did it yourself
it's time to relax now
and then give it hell

someday you'll find
what you're lookin' for
someday you'll find
what you're lookin' for

you didn't bet on the dodgers
to beat the giants
then david came up
now you gotta pay up
you didn't count on that

geez half the money's gone
the month is still young
where you gonna go now?
things are closin' in

got to trust someone
trust someone
someone you trust
got to be careful
be careful

you can't go to your brother
that money's all gone
can't go to your friends

someday
you'll find
everything you're lookin' for

someday
you'll find
everything you're lookin' for

made out like a bandit
for so many years
what are you workin' for?
one more big score?
what are you tryin' to prove?

try to get closer
but not too close
try to get through
but not be through

no one can touch you now
but i can touch you now
you're invisible
you got too many secrets
bob dylan said that
somethin' like that

someday
you'll find
everything you're lookin' for

someday
you'll find
everything you're lookin' for

bandit

earl was a painter and a vietnam vet. there's a lot of those. he specialized in psychedelic paintings. he painted a lot. sun used to love to watch him. he was not a very successful painter and he never did sell anything, but he always tried. he took them to gallery L on main street. lenore was the owner of the gallery. he was always getting turned down.

bandit

when the instrumental happens there at the end when i was playing the guitar, the devil went to earl's studio. he went to his studio and materialized there and cleaned earl's glasses. he cleaned his glasses.

bandit

when the devil cleaned earl's glasses he laid them down there by the easel and he left. then earl came in the next day, put on his glasses and started painting stuff he'd never painted before. suddenly, he was painting this picture of this guy in a red suit with red shoes and kind of a panama hat with a red hatband on it, holding a sign that said "alaska" on it, like he was hitchhiking. and he's going "i've never painted anything like this before," so he took it to the gallery to see what would happen and lenore, who runs the gallery, she loved it. she loved this painting. she hung it in the most prominent place in the gallery and told earl to bring in anything he painted and that she would love to have it. it was the most fantastic thing that ever happened to earl. and he couldn't figure it out, but what the heck, huh? got a painting in there now....i tell you all of this because you can't tell by listening to the songs, you have to listen to the instrumentals to get this. anyway, so when you see somebody like eric clapton up there playing guitar and closing his eyes it could be anything. it could be anything.

grandpa's interview

earl, what a guy, huh? well a lot of things are going on. jed's in jail. sun doesn't know what's going on because jed's in jail and he used to be the youngest person in the family she could talk to....now the media is out of control, i think we all know that. it's nice to have them with us, but not always. they're a little pushy. so they came to interview grandpa about jed. because jed killed a cop, of course they wanna do a special about that....let's find out what the green family thinks. wow! that's the wrong guitar, i can't do that. i'm trying to remember what key this is in. i put them down, it's got big numbers and letters so i can see them, not that i'm like grandpa. but who cares what chapter this is. only people on the internet. you people will have to get tapes of other shows, well, i don't have to talk to you directly, you're not here. i'm trying to adapt to technology....2k3, here we are. when i was writing these songs and recording them, we had no idea what was going on. grandpa was my favorite and when he died, i mean he had a, whatever happened, a heart attack or something....that really blew my mind. i was not ready for that. it was unfortunate. and among the guys in the studio, when i went by there that morning and we recorded that song, everybody was depressed. but we liked him. he always had something funny to say. everything he said was funny. but he was so serious that you couldn't tell how funny it was until later. so, that was a sad, sad thing. it was a surprise....you can't think....so, i'm gonna write a song about grandpa and he's gonna die. you have to let it come out. just started and kept on going, recorded the first one and then i wrote the second one. that's when i realized the same characters were in the second song as were in the first song. it was a big surprise. we were all keeping track of it. it was kind of like watching a soap opera or something. every day i'd come in with a new song. usually wrote it on the way over there. i'd stop my car and write a little bit. then when it stopped coming i'd move my car about 500 yards and stop again. there was a whole bunch more material there. so i wrote that down too. anyway, it's too bad. 'cause i liked grandpa.

grandpa's interview

"grandpa, here's your coffee"
said edith as she filled his cup,
"nobody'll find you here
and earl is glad you guys showed up

the way things are downtown
you might have to stay for a while
there was a helicopter flyin' over your house
when i talked to your neighbor kyle"

"who the hell do they think they are
invading our home like that?
grandma and i had to leave so fast
we couldn't even catch the cat

the helicopter scared the shit out of it
and it took off down the trail
down past the railroad track
towards the county jail"

"jed you really screwed up now
what'd you have to do that for?
everybody wants to hang your ass
and here's a note from lenore"

she touched the cold steel bars
as she pushed the paper in
jed took it up and read it
and he couldn't hide a grin

outside the jail window
a crow flew across the sky
completely disappearing behind each bar
then a helicopter flew by

"say hi to earl and edith
tell 'em i'm doin' fine
tell 'em you're ready to leave home now
and they should cut the line

can't grandma come and see me?
i've got a new song to sing
it's longer than all the others combined
and it doesn't mean a thing"

the noise was unfamiliar...
a walkie talkie squealed
generators were runnin'
vans parked in the field

tv crews and cameras
they wanted to interview grandpa on the porch
they came through the gate and up on the lawn
knockin' down edith's tiki torch

grandpa saw them there
lookin' through the venetian blind
"those people don't have any respect
so they won't get any of mine

i ain't gonna talk about jed...
i don't watch channel 2 or 6 or 9
i don't have time to talk that fast
and it ain't my crime

it ain't an honor to be on tv
and it ain't a duty either
the only good thing about tv
is shows like 'leave it to beaver'

shows with love and affection
like mama used to say
'a little mayberry livin'
can go a long way'"

he took earl's gun down from the closet
and loaded up both barrels
went out on the porch and fired them off
and up walked a woman named carol

"susan carol from early magazine
i've got some questions to ask"

"well you can stick 'em where the sun don't shine"
grandpa said with a gasp

then he fell face first and let out a sigh
edith came out in shock
grandpa was whispering to her from down on the floor
he looked like he was tryin' to talk

"that guy who just keeps singin'
can't somebody shut him up?
i don't know for the life of me
where he comes up with this stuff"

they laid his head on a newspaper
with a picture of carmichael on the front page
posing with a little league baseball team
and a seedy shot of jed with a motorcycle

grandpa died like a hero
fightin' for freedom of silence
tryin' to stop the media
tryin' to be anonymous

share your lovin' and you live so long
share your lovin' and you live so long
share your lovin' and you live so long
live so long

bringin' down dinner
so when grandpa died, it was a surprise to everybody. i'm sorry, i wish it had been a happier story up to this point. but we still have youth. we still have youth on our side. living in that house is that beautiful little girl, ready to break out. and right now grandma's driving around, they've got this car, it's a huge white eldorado, a '78 eldorado. it's very big and very wide. so we came in and put down that track and it was a long one. and when we got to the end of it, my friend ralph walked over and looked at the lyric sheet and said, "grandpa's dead!" and everybody was kind of realizing that at once and he was our favorite character. it was kind of too bad, because he was the only one that was really funny. so we were kind of depressed. i came by the next day and everybody's standing around and i didn't have a song. i usually write songs on the way over, but this time i didn't have one, even though i stopped at all the right places in the car and opened the door and took out my piece of paper and pen. i couldn't write, nothing happened...it reminded me of when i was about 3 years old and i went up in the attic to see my daddy, who's a writer. he's written many books. he had an old underwood typewriter. i walked up there and it took a lot of nerve to go up there, because you weren't supposed to go up there 'cause he was writing, so i walked over and i looked up at him and i said, "what're you doing, daddy?" and he said, "well, i'm writing," and i looked up at him and said, "what're you writing?" he said, "i don't know." he said, "i just come up here every day and start writing, sometimes i don't write anything, sometimes i write all day. i don't know what i'm writing," i said "well" to myself, "there must be something to learn there." my 3-year-old brain was churning on overtime. so i went back downstairs. one morning i woke up, it was the third day, after i'd told the guys, "we must be done, we might as well go home because i don't know what's gonna happen now." and then i thought, "what about grandma? what happened to grandma?"

bringin' down dinner

the evening fog was rollin' in
it was getting hard to see
the old white car edged down the road
headed for the double e

she was bringin' down dinner for grandpa
it was crawlin' with vitamins
and tender as a mother's love
when she saw the tv vans

the side door was open
there were three tv's
grandpa's face was on every one
he was talkin' to a woman with a microphone
she was sexy and her hair was all done

sun green came out and met grandma then
"my, you're such a beautiful girl
mother earth needs more like you
you should go out now and see the world

what's grandpa doin' on tv?
i got his dinner in the car
all these vans have blocked our road
but we can carry it, it's not too far"

sun green

well, they had a wake for grandpa. they put him in a chair in the living room. all his friends came by and started talking to him. everybody said what they wanted to say. as per grandpa's instructions, the funeral home used all their oldest cars. brought them in front of the double E and they were all there: old '50s american cars, whitewalls, black cars. the next day sun green got up and packed her bags and left home. you know how it is when you're a kid, you're trying to say something but you can't get it out. somebody you're trying to talk to, some older person, maybe your parents, they keep talking to you, they don't stop. you want to say something but you just can't. what a situation....well, an airplane was flying by. out in the field, sun looked up and saw it. she'd just finished her project. she was hoping that people could look out the window of the airplane and see what she'd made. she had made a huge circle in straw about 200 feet across. the line creating the circle was about three feet wide, so it was a lot of straw she had to put down to create this huge circle. in the middle of circle in straw on the beautiful green grass, the wheat-colored straw spelled out "war." and then a huge line went diagonally through it in straw, crossing it out. she was looking at it from her pickup truck, very happy with herself for making a statement. for an 18-year-old to make a statement like that is a great feeling. and she was proud of herself. she decided to go into greendale and see jed in jail, see how he was doin', talk to him, take him something. i'm sorry i wish it had been a happier story up to this point. but we still have youth. like i said before, i don't think there can be a better feeling than youth making a difference.

sun green

sun green started makin' waves
on the day her grandpa died
speakin' out against anything
unjust or packed with lies

she chained herself to a statue of an eagle
in the lobby of powerco
and started yellin' through a megaphone
"there's corruption on the highest floor"

suits poured out of elevators   *"they're all dirty"*
phoneheads began to speak   *"you can't trust anybody"*

but security couldn't get her down
she was welded to the eagle's beak

sun green leaned into that megaphone
said, *"truth is all i seek"*
security brought in some blowtorches
news cameras recorded the speech

"when the city is plunged into darkness
by an unpredicted rolling blackout
the white house always blames the governor
sayin' 'the solution is to vote him out'"

on top of that great bronze eagle
sun's voice was loud and clear
she said *"powerco is workin' with the white house*
to paralyze our state with fear"

it was a golden moment
in the history of tv news
no one could explain it
it just got great reviews

*"hey mr. clean, you're dirty now too
hey mr. clean, you're dirty now too
hey mr. clean, you're dirty now too
hey mr. clean, you're dirty now too"*

the imitators were playin'
down at john lee's bar
when sun went down to see 'em
someone followed her in a car

so now when she goes dancin'
she has to watch her back
the fbi just trashed her room
one of them kicked her cat

the damn thing scratched his leg
and he had to shoot it dead
and leave it lyin' in a puddle of blood
at the foot of sun green's bed

"hey mr. clean, you're dirty now too
hey mr. clean, you're dirty now too
hey mr. clean, you're dirty now too
hey mr. clean, you're dirty now too"

john lee's was rockin'
the imitators drove it home
sun was dancin' up a heatwave
for a while she was all alone...

when up walked a tall stranger
he shadowed her move to move
in perfect unison
a supernatural groove

he took her by the hand
and the room began to spin
he said "i'm earth...earth brown
you know the shape i'm in

i'm leavin' tonight for alaska
and i want you to come in the spring
and be a goddess in the planet wars
tryin' to save the livin' things"

"i'm ready to go right now"
sun green told earth brown
"let's go back to my place
pick up my cat and leave this town behind"

"hey mr. clean, you're dirty now too
hey mr. clean, you're dirty now too
hey mr. clean, you're dirty now too
hey mr. clean, you're dirty now too"

next day sun green got busted for pot
and it made the headline news
but then the charges all got dropped
and the story got confused

she'd still like to meet julia butterfly
and see what remedy brings
and be a goddess in the planet wars
tryin' to save the livin' things

but that might not be easy
livin' on the run
mother earth has many enemies
there's much work to be done

"hey mr. clean, you're dirty now too
hey mr. clean, you're dirty now too
hey mr. clean, you're dirty now too
hey mr. clean, you're dirty now too"

be the rain

so sun met earth brown in john lee's bar. earth was fascinated and captivated by her beauty, the symmetry of her moves. he couldn't take his eyes off her. while he was watching her, the devil came up behind him. he saw that earth was drinking some alaska water, from the glaciers. the devil put some devil dust in earth's bottle of water, just dropped a little in there. the water started glowing, shining, turning red and then it turned silver. the devil poisoned earth....earth was still watching sun dance. shadows were all over the place. it was the most amazing thing he'd ever seen. he walked right up and introduced himself and they left together for alaska....he started thinking too much, second-guessing. nothing happened that he didn't question and then question again. his thirst was overwhelming. he and sun were in the alaskan camper, headed north on highway 1 to alaska. earth stopped at a convenience store and bought several cartons of water. he kept about a dozen bottles in the front seat and put the rest of it in the back. there was a strange red glow in the back. he noticed it, but he forgot about it so fast. he thought he heard a noise in the engine, though....the engine was making funny sounds. the windshield wipers weren't working right. they were flying up highway 1. earth was sweating. sun was peacefully asleep, with her head resting on his shoulder, not a care in the world. she was dreaming. she was dreaming about a high school play....she was onstage. there was a big cardboard house on the stage, looked just like the double E. there was a light coming out of the window where sun's window was. there was a yellow light coming out and it shone down on her on the stage. grandpa was sitting on the porch in his rocking chair. on the other side of the stage there was a cardboard jail. jed was sitting there talking to officer carmichael. sun's cat walked across the stage. then the cheerleaders all came out, but they looked different. they had camouflage outfits on, raggy, dirty camouflage. they had bandanas in camouflage and war paint on their faces. they were waving a big camouflage flag with a black monkey wrench on it. sun looked at herself: she was dressed in camouflage, too. she had a little army hat on and a bandana around her forehead, war paint on her cheeks. the imitators started playing and sun picked up her megaphone.

be the rain

save the planet for another day
   "attention shoppers, buy with a conscience and save"
save the planet for another day
   "save alaska! let the caribou stay"
don't care what the governments say
   "they're all bought and paid for anyway"
save the planet for another day
   "hey big oil, what do you say?"

we were runnin' through the night
never knowin' if we would see the light
paranoid schizophrenic visions
livin' in fear of the wrong decisions

we got to wake up
we got to keep goin'
if they follow us
there's no way of knowin'

we got a job to do
we got to
save mother earth

be the ocean when it meets the sky
   "you can make a difference, if you really try"
be the magic in the northern lights
   "six days...six nights"
be the river as it rolls along
   "it has three-eyed fish and it's smellin' strong"
be the rain you remember fallin'
   "be the rain, be the rain"

yeah rain was fallin' and we're soakin' wet
hail is beatin' down on our heads
the wind is blowin' through our hair
faces frozen in the frigid air

we got to get there
alaska
we got to be there
before the big machines

we got a job to do
we got to
save mother earth

dream the hunter on the western plain
   "the birds are all gone, where did they go?"
dream the fisherman in his boat
   "he's comin' home empty, he's barely afloat"
dream the logger in the great northwest
   "they're runnin' out of trees, they got to give it a rest
   (there's no other way to cut it)"
dream the farmer in the old heartland
   "corporate greed and chemicals are killin' the land"

next mornin' sun was up at dawn
she looked around and earth was gone

dark visions he had last night
he needed peace, he needed light

he heard the rumble and
he saw the big machines
the green army rose
it was a bad dream

he had a job to do
he had to
save mother earth

be the ocean when it meets the sky
    "greek freighters are dumping crap somewhere right now"
be the magic in the northern lights
    "the ice is melting!"
be the river as it rolls along
    "toxic waste dumpin' from corporate farms"
be the rain you remember fallin'
    "be the rain, be the rain"
save the planet for another day
    "be the rain, be the rain"
be the river as it rolls along
    "be the rain, be the rain"

jay

m

maha

col. jackson green
married
sally o'day

capt. john green
married
ciela oaks

stone green
married
misty alder

sky green
married
terra locust

jed green

jacob green

sun gr

DOUBLE E RANCH

the green

n

ross

arius green (grandpa)

married

ciela oaks

married

close thibodeaux

rl green

hill green

sea green

carling green

narried

h o'riley

luna green

mily tree

Jay Carling Green

Born November 11, 1895, Treasure, Idaho. Started work as a Yard grunt for the Western Pacific Railway, worked up to an engineer before he left the company in 1925 to make his living by shipping potatoes on the railway. Founded the Green Transport Company in 1927. Moved to Greendale 1931. Died Nov. 1963.

Mahalia Cross

Born June, 1898, Valentine, Idaho. Employed as a barmaid in the Valentine Hotel, until she married Jay Carling Green in 1923. She gave him three sons: Jackson, Arius and John. Mahalia Green is still living in Greendale.

Jackson Jay Green

Born 1923, Treasure, Idaho. Joined the U.S. Air Force at 18 years, fought in WW2 and Korea. Rose to rank of Colonel in 1951. Moved to Lake Tahoe, CA, 1956. Disabled in military accident in Utah, 1961. Retired from military with Honorable Discharge. Started Green Boating Company in Lake Tahoe, 1963, selling Garwood runabouts and designing wooden raceboats until his retirement in 1985, famous in the art for his revolutionary methods of tuning speed boat hulls and motors to attain highest performance. A legendary name in fresh water wooden race boat history.

Sally Tulsa O'Day

Born 1926, Valentine, Idaho, daughter of Mike O'Day, Idaho potato champion known for unique ability to grow more potatoes in an acre than was thought possible at the time, and Beauty Masterson, out of wedlock. Mike and Beauty were later married in 1930. Sally O'Day married Jackson Green in 1945 and gave him one son, Stone. She died in a car accident, Lake Tahoe, 1956.

Stone Green

Born November 1, 1946, Treasure, Idaho, joined army at 18, rose to rank of sergeant, fought in Vietnam War, moved to Greendale, CA in 1967, died in 1976 after a long illness possibly of complications from extreme exposure to Agent Orange in Vietnam.

Misty Alder

Born 1946, Crow, Texas, married Stone Green in 1964 and gave him two sons, Jed and Jacob. Died at her own hand, 1976.

Jed Green

Born 1969, Greendale, CA, taken into foster home at age 7, after mother's death in 1976. Raised by foster parents, Giovanni and Lenore Randazzo, in Greendale, CA.

Capt. John Green

Born 1924, Treasure, Idaho, served in the U.S. Navy in the Korean War 1950, decorated for bravery by President Eisenhower. Started Green Marine Shipping Company in 1955.

Jacob Green

Born 1971, Greendale, CA, taken into foster home at age 5, after mother's death in 1976. Raised by foster parents, Mark and June Carmichael, moved to San Diego, CA, 1980. Entire family drowned in 1982 boating accident off the coast of San Clemente, CA.

Sky Bleu Green

Born 1945, San Francisco, CA, graduated high school 1963, moved to Hawaii to study marine biology at the University of Hawaii. Worked with dolphins and whales, researching communication with mammals and fishes, became legendary for her ability to "call" dolphins, sharks and whales. Married Professor Terra Beach Locust in 1975. Became interested in extra-terrestrial life and contacts reported in a triangle between the Big Island of Hawaii, the island Maui and an unspecified point on the floor of the Pacific Ocean. Skilled at deep water diving without tanks, Sky was known to stay submerged for unusually long periods of time. Moved with Terra to the Island of Hawaii in 1999, where he developed and practiced his healing skills, based on gentle manipulation of outer skin to relieve shadows of old injuries from past lives. In 1982, Sky gave Terra twin daughters, Sola and Ciela. Sky and Terra Locust still reside on the Big Island.

Ciela Bleu Oaks

Born 1927, Paris, France, daughter of California winemaker Sylvan Oaks, moved to Napa, CA in 1940. Known for her powers with animals and ability to communicate with plants, Ciela was at once revered and feared by the Napa community. Ciela strongly opposed the use of chemicals on grape vines, which was just catching on when her family became involved in the Napa wine business. On more than one occasion, strange animal and plant behaviors directly altering wine production were attributed to Ciela's powers. She disappeared abruptly in San Francisco in 1965, while on an afternoon visit to the Botanical Gardens. Her fate is a mystery to this day. The case was never closed. Married John Green in 1944 and divorced in 1945.* She gave him one daughter, Sky. *See (Arius Green/Ciela)

Arius Jay Green

Born 1928, Treasure, Idaho, worked as a brakeman for the Western Pacific Railroad, saw no military service because of poor vision, invested in stock market and made millions of dollars, which he reinvested in the Western Pacific. He became a prominent shareholder in the company, influencing its direction and growth during the late '40s and '50s. Widely respected for his candid opinions and strong direction, Arius Green was seen as one of the fathers of the Western Pacific. Took residence in San Francisco, CA and moved to Greendale, CA in 1961. Retired in 1988.

Earl Green

Born 1947, San Francisco, CA, drafted at age 19, served in the Vietnam war. Following his term of duty, Earl became an artist and took up residence in Greendale, CA.

Edith Morgan O'Riley

Born 1952, Lake Tahoe, CA, the daughter of meat processor and financier Tom O'Riley. Edith's mother, Claudette, was a founder of the famous "pink ladies" who continue to this day to help in hospitals around California by making sick patients feel at home, especially those without family, by donating their time, and augmenting hospital staff. Edith was a popular singer in Lake Tahoe, sharing her folk music with others at local spots. Known as a natural dancer, she was a wonder to behold, legendary in the Tahoe area for starting a good time everywhere she went. Her dance movements have been compared to a deer moving at the speed of a hummingbird on occasion. She was known and loved for her music and dance throughout the region. She made one recording, "Don't Fence Me In," which became a regional hit in South Dakota, maintaining the #1 position on the radio in Zeona, South Dakota for almost one year. She married Earl Green in 1978, and gave him twin daughters, Sun and Luna.

Sun Ciela Green

Born 1984, Greendale, CA, a bright student, she placed near the top of her class consistently through high school. Known for her graceful dancing skills, acrobatic prowess, and highly developed sense of balance, she could easily climb up and down sheer walls and ancient Sequoia redwood trees with the use of ropes. At a young age it was noticed that Sun was able to "call in" the cows at roundup time without the use of Australian shepherd herding dogs, widely used for that purpose in Greendale and surrounding area pastures. Her ability to "tame" bulls and predict accurately the number of eggs the chickens would lay earned her an early reputation as naturally gifted. As she grew into her teens, she became more concerned with the environment and the planet Earth, organizing "Earth Day" rallies at Greendale High School. She was a cheerleader, but was not overly proud of that accomplishment according to her friends at the time.

Luna Ciela Green

Born 1984, Greendale, CA, died 1984. Soon after birth fell victim of an unknown disease of the heart, similar to that affecting a herd of buffalo, transported to the Greendale area from Wyoming that year. That same year, a herd of caribou came down with the fatal disease in Alaska, and 51 whales beached themselves and died of the disease in Hawaii. No other humans were known to have been victims of the disease.

Hill Green

Born 1948, San Francisco, CA, a large boy, with a strong artistic tendency, Hill was drafted into military service in 1966. He went to Vietnam where he died serving his country.

Sea Green

Born 1950, in San Francisco, CA, known for her powers with animals and plants, was an explorer from her earliest years. At 10 years she became lost in Sequoia National Forest while on a family vacation and was assumed dead. However, she was found by forest rangers after six weeks, in perfect health, suffering no injuries. Park authorities were able to learn little of her six week experience. At seventeen, Sea traveled to Alaska on a school trip to study the wilderness. She was lost again and was never found.

Close Wanda Thibodeaux

Born 1949, Lafayette, LA, parentage unknown, lived with an Indian tribe in the midwest for some of her first 18 years. Self-educated, Close practiced her effective use of herbal remedies. Her knowledge of Indian cures was applied successfully on many ill people, and she was known as a gifted healer. She married Arius Jay Green in 1970 and gave him one son, Carling.

Carling SnowBear Green

Born 1971, Greendale, CA, joined the U.S. Air Force as a communications expert in 1989, served in Iraq, moved from Greendale to Technopolis, CA in 1992, made millions of dollars in the Information Technology industry by founding a successful internet company, and lost it all in the subsequent market crash. Carling is now working as a salesperson at a used car dealership in Nome, Alaska.

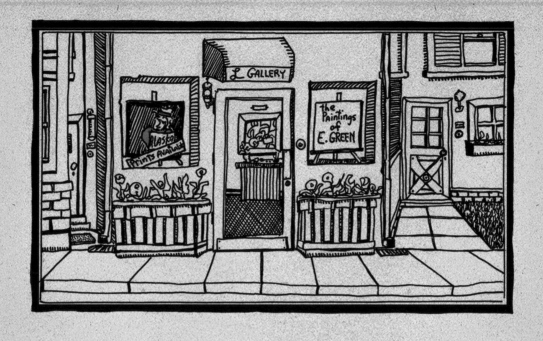

the earl green
collection

by james mazzeo

a circumference of circumstance

12' w x 9' h, fluorescent acrylic, 2002

a circumference of circumstance

12' w x 9' h, fluorescent acrylic, 2002

(black light)

pink eye

36" w x 48" h, fluorescent acrylic, 2002

pink eye

36" w x 48" h, fluorescent acrylic, 2002

(black light)

swimming with humans

48" w x 30" h, fluorescent acrylic, 2002

swimming with humans

48" w x 30" h, fluorescent acrylic, 2002

(black light)

route 66

36" w x 36" h, fluorescent acrylic, 2002

route 66

36" w x 36" h, fluorescent acrylic, 2002

(black light)

dekooning with capers

40" w x 30" h, fluorescent acrylic, 2002

dekooning with capers

40" w x 30" h, fluorescent acrylic, 2002

(black light)

the gumption of my assumption

24" w x 36" h, fluorescent acrylic, 2002

the gumption of my assumption

24" w x 36" h, fluorescent acrylic, 2002

(black light)

module

30” w x 36” h, fluorescent acrylic, 2001

module

30" w x 36" h, fluorescent acrylic, 2001

(black light)

pacific lettuce
30" w x 30" h, fluorescent acrylic, 2000

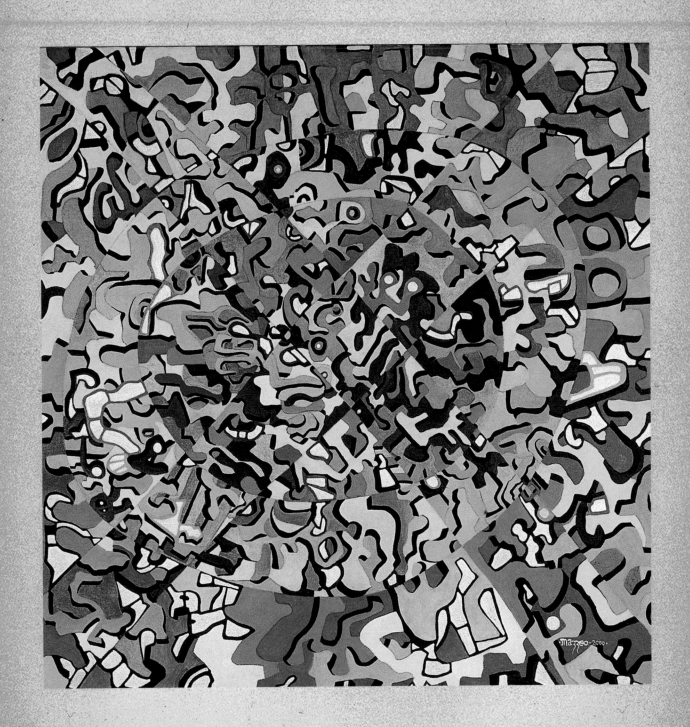

pacific lettuce

30" w x 30" h, fluorescent acrylic, 2000

(black light)

in for no

24" w x 30" h, fluorescent acrylic, 2000

in for no

24" w x 30" h, fluorescent acrylic, 2000

(black light)

repose
36" w x 48" h, fluorescent acrylic, 2001

repose

36" w x 48" h, fluorescent acrylic, 2001

(black light)

the successful irradication of your local hot spot

48" w x 36" h, fluorescent acrylic, 2001

the successful irradication of your local hot spot

48" w x 36" h, fluorescent acrylic, 2001

(black light)

mind's eye

18" w x 24" h, fluorescent acrylic, 1994

Mazzeo ·1994·

mind's eye

18" w x 24" h, fluorescent acrylic, 1994

(black light)

the artist

james mazzeo

1944   Born Oakland, California

1958-62   Mazzeo's art teacher, John Quigley was a big influence on him. In his senior year Quigley entered three of Mazzeo's paintings in a major show of more than 700 artists. All three received awards in the Valley Fair amateur art contest: "Best of Show", "Honorable Mention" and "First Place—Abstract Art" for tissue paper collage. The interest level generated at this show initiated the first sales of his artworks.

1966   Creates a one man "Light Show".

1967   Andy Warhol and his light show joined forces with Mazzeo's light show in order to fill a large theatre in Boston, Mass. They played together for four nights with The Velvet Underground and Nico. Mazzeo is invited to join the "Living Arts" program at the Fogg Museum at Harvard University.

1969   Attends Cañada College in Woodside, California where he writes and publishes a student poetry magazine called "Live-Evil".

1971   Creates set designs and costume designs for Neil Young's "Journey Through The Past".

1975   Illustrates the album cover and song book for Neil Young's "Zuma".

1989   Designs a major new light show for Neil Young's "Lost Dogs" tour of Japan, Australia and New Zealand. This new light show is called "Traveling Light". His paintings and drawings are loosely animated through multiple projectors and seem to dance along with the music.

1990   Moto Haru Sano, a very popular Japanese singer/songwriter, asks Mazzeo to design a light show to travel with his 90-show tour of Japan. This light show is called "Napoleon Fish" and is a huge success across Japan.

1999   Has his first one man show in Woodside, California.

2001   Paints a series called "Fucking With Picasso" (Picasso by blacklight).

2002   Paints a 9' tall and 12' wide nine-panel piece entitled "Circumference of Circumstance".

2003   Mazzeo designs and builds cardboard stage sets for Neil Young's "Greendale" film. Cardboard trucks, cars, houses, the jail and a large map of Alaska are shown throughout the movie. He also does all pen and ink drawings illustrating the story of Greendale for the stage play and the album packaging.

2004   Creates all original pen and ink artworks of Greendale for publication in the hard cover book "Greendale" by Neil Young.

Recent and current exhibitions:
   The Linc Gallery, San Francisco, Ca.
   The Lowe Gallery, Santa Monica, Ca.

Collections:
   Joe Baker, Santa Cruz, Ca.
   Genevieve Bujold, Malibu, Ca.
   Greg Coben, Santa Cruz, Ca.
   Eric Clapton, London, England
   Alexander Djerassi, Woodside, Ca.
   Dale Djerassi, Woodside, Ca.
   The Esalen Institute, Big Sur, Ca.
   Kimberly Hemphill, South Miami Beach, Fla.
   Michael Johnson, Santa Cruz, Ca.
   John Lydon, Woodside, Ca.
   Sir Robert Maxwell Collection, London, England
   Christine & Michelle Montez, Fremont, Ca.
   James McCracken, Deer Isle, Me.
   Joel Radman, Philadelphia, Miss.
   Elliot Roberts, Malibu, Ca.
   Linda Ronstadt, Tucson, Ariz.
   Frank Sampedro, Los Angeles, Ca.
   Moto Haru Sano, Tokyo, Japan
   Roger Sommers, Mill Valley, Ca.
   Jeff Trusso, San Jose, Ca.
   Alan Watts, Muir Woods, Ca.
   Neil & Pegi Young, Woodside, Ca.
   Zeke & Jessica Young, Los Angeles, Ca.
   Raza Zaidi & Amy Trusso, San Francisco, Ca.

sacred cow

36" w x 24" h, acrylic on canvas, 1994

aluna

48" w x 36" h, acrylic on canvas, 1994

don't forget to water the cactus

36" w x 48" h, acrylic on canvas, 1994

vienna woods

30" w x 40" h, acrylic on canvas, 1996

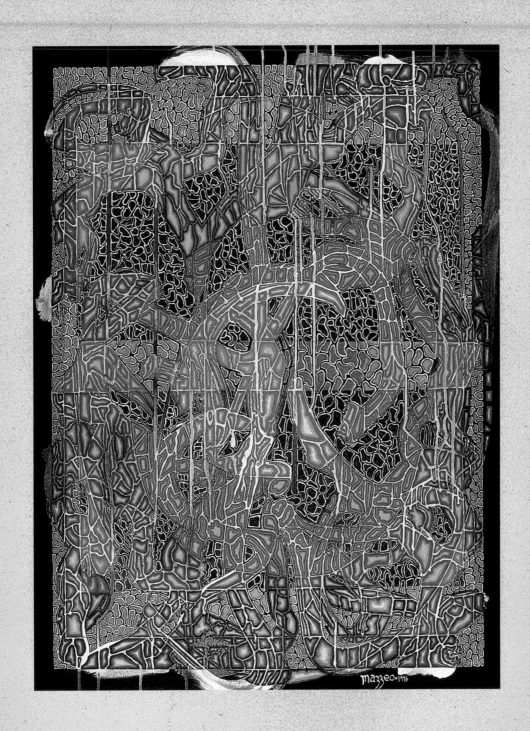

tequila moon

30" w x 40" h, acrylic on canvas, 1995

fourteen very blue balls

40" w x 30" h, acrylic on canvas, 2000

whale fire

48" w x 36" h, acrylic on canvas, 1996

rumour

24" w x 20" h, oil & gesso on canvas, 1990

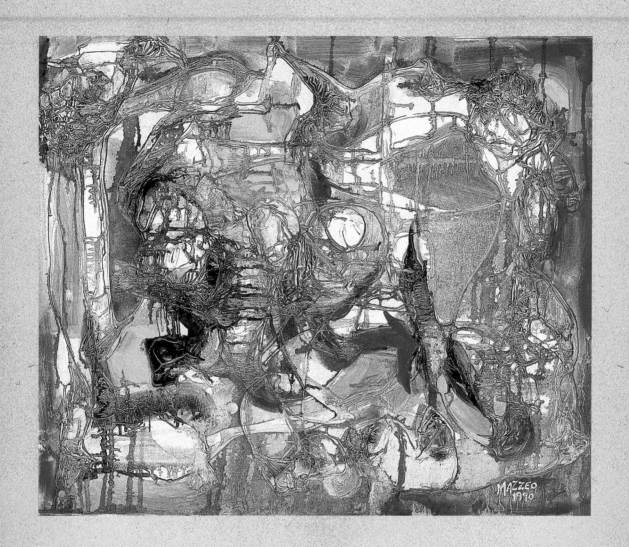

night of the comet

40" w x 30" h, acrylic on canvas, 1997

lady bug

24" w x 36" h, acrylic on canvas, 1997